The Revelation

OF LIFE AFTER DEATH BEFORE THE CROSS, and AFTER THE CROSS

The Revelation of Life After Death Before the Cross, and After the Cross
Copyright © 2023 by Waymon J Marshall

Published in the United States of America

ISBN   Paperback: 979-8-89091-263-3
ISBN   eBook: 979-8-89091-264-0

All rights reserved. No part of this publication may be reproduced, stored in a retrieval system or transmitted in any way by any means, electronic, mechanical, photocopy, recording or otherwise without the prior permission of the author except as provided by USA copyright law.

The opinions expressed by the author are not necessarily those of ReadersMagnet, LLC.

ReadersMagnet, LLC
10620 Treena Street, Suite 230 | San Diego, California, 92131 USA
1.619. 354. 2643 | www.readersmagnet.com

Book design copyright © 2023 by ReadersMagnet, LLC. All rights reserved.

Cover design by Tiffany Curaza
Interior design by Daniel Lopez

THE Revelation

OF LIFE AFTER DEATH BEFORE THE CROSS, and AFTER THE CROSS

A Peek into Hell, and a Glimpse into Glory

Amazing Mysteries of:
Eternity, Paradise, Abraham's Bosom,
and the Place of Torment

WAYMON J MARSHALL

Preface

I would like to thank GOD, the FATHER, for His plan, the LORD JESUS CHRIST for carrying out the Plan, and the HOLY SPIRIT for His indwelling presence and power in my life, not only mine but all believers. I would like to thank my wife, Donna, and my son, Steven, for putting up with all the times I had messy papers everywhere. I would like to thank my two sisters and brother-in-law, Dorothy Kearns, and Joyce, and Tarl Lloyd for their help in proofreading, typing, correcting misspelled words, and helping to organize this project. Thanks to Janice and James Campbell for their inspiration and support. Thanks also to Margaret and T. D. Hodge, my friend and brother in Christ, who taught me to depend on the Holy Spirit to bring things of God to my remembrance and to guide me, and also because we all get older and have trouble finding things, so the taught me to ask the Holy Spirit for help. Because He is omnipresent, He will help. The Bible says we receive not, because we ask not. Last of all, I thank my college basketball friend and his wife, Walter and Pat Brown, who is truly a family that has a powerful and true testimony of God's love, miracles, mercy, and grace.

Lord Jesus, "Let the words of my mouth and meditation of my heart be acceptable in your sight, O, Lord my strength and redeemer." Psalm 19:14

Bible verses from King James Version

In the Old Testament, death is revealed only in shadows and mysteries. From Genesis to Ecclesiastes, not clearly revealing what happens at death, we only know that there is a separation of the soul and the spirit from the physical body at death, but where do this soul and spirit go? The first few pages' reveal what the Bible says about death from Genesis to Ecclesiastes. The next pictures, I pray, will help reveal what JESUS, the Creator of all things in heaven and earth, reveals in Luke 16:19–31. JESUS reveals what happened to a certain beggar, a type of believer, and a certain rich man, a type of unbeliever, two people who actually lived on earth, then died and had two different destinations. Most Bible scholars believe this is a parable, but check the biblical record, and you will find that JESUS never used personal names in any of the parable He gave. In this story, He mentions Lazarus, Abraham and Moses, and the prophets. The definition of a parable is an earthly story with a heavenly meaning. Abraham and Moses were real people and mentioned throughout the Bible.

THE REVELATION OF LIFE AFTER DEATH BEFORE THE CROSS, AND AFTER THE CROSS

Artist's Name: Gordon Thompson, May 2005

Scripture: Luke 16:19–31; Luke 23:32; Luke 23:39–43; Matthew 12:40; Matthew 27:50–52: 1 Peter 4:6; and Ephesians 4:8–10

Scriptures from: King James Version

The artist drew these amazing pictures by biblical descriptions from what I (Waymon Marshall) wrote in the details of what I wanted in the pictures. Gordon has an amazing God-given gift. For example, the very first picture was drawn from a house that we rode around to find so that he could get the idea of what I wanted revealed in the first drawing. The house had to have a big picture window for the rich man to look out and see Lazarus laying at his gate begging for crumbs.

May this information enlighten your spiritual understanding of what God has revealed about life after death in the Bible. God bless.

Glossary of Terms

Judgment Seat of Christ: Judgement of believers' works. Not for salvation because it was purchased at the cross by Jesus by His death, burial, and resurrection, but for rewards and crowns, for our works and service for Christ. 2 Corinthians 5:10

Gathered to thy Fathers: Old Testament term for the death of the righteous being united with their dead (righteous) relatives in Abraham's bosom. Luke 16:19–31 (Other references shown on next two pages).

Third Heaven–2 Corinthians 12:1–4: *(1) It is not expedient for me doubtless to glory. I will come to visions and revelations of the Lord. (2) I knew a man above fourteen years ago, (whether in the body, I cannot tell; or whether out of the body, I cannot tell: God knoweth;) such a one caught up in the third heaven. (3) And I knew such a man, (whether in the body or out the body, I cannot tell: God knoweth). (4) How that he was caught up into paradise, and heard unspeakable words, which it is not lawful for a man to utter.* Paul was speaking of himself being caught up in the 3rd heaven called paradise. Possibly when he was stoned at Antioch in Acts 14, *And there came thither certain Jews from Antioch and Iconium, who persuaded the people, and having stoned Paul, drew him out of the city, supposing he had been dead, Howbeit, as the disciples stood round about him, he rose up, and came into the city: and the next day he departed with Barnabas to Derbe* (Acts 14:19–20).

Rapture: Period of time when Jesus calls all believers, living and dead to meet Him in the air and be taken to heaven.

THE REVELATION OF LIFE AFTER DEATH BEFORE THE CROSS, AND AFTER THE CROSS

Eternity: Endless, infinite, or immeasurable state of existence after physical death whether in heaven, hell, New Jerusalem, or the lake of fire.

Hell: The nether world of the unrighteous dead which the unrighteous dead continue to exist after the physical body dies. Their five sense continue to operate in a world of hopelessness, torment, fire, and mental punishment. (Revelation 21:11–27; Luke 16:23–26)

Abraham's Bosom (Paradise): The holding place or prison for the righteous dead before the cross, an enclosure to house the righteous, a type of paradise. After Jesus' resurrection, the people located in this paradise were moved to the heavenly paradise in the 3rd heaven. (Revelation chapters 21 and 22)

Great White Throne: Final judgement of all the unrighteous dead whether they died in the sea, death and hell gives up the dead that were in them for this judgement for works (Revelation 20:11–15). The beast and the false prophet will also be cast into this lake of fire in Revelation 20:14 and also the devil in Revelation 20:10.

Book of Works: Books that record the life of all souls born, according to their works (Revelation 19:11–15).

Lamb's Book of Life: Book that records all the deeds of all who put their trust in the Lord and Savior, Jesus Christ. It is possible to be recorded in the Book of Works and not be recorded in the Lamb's Book of Life because of their rejection of Jesus as their Lord and Savior, alone for their eternal destination (Revelation 19:15).

Saved or Born Again: State of being redeemed from being dead in trespasses and sin, to being purchased to eternal life by the precious blood of Jesus. But if we walk in the light, as (Jesus) is in the light, we have fellowship one with another, and the blood of Jesus Christ, His son, cleanses us from all sin. If we say that we have no sin, we deceive ourselves, and the truth is not in us. If we confess our sins, he is faithful and just to forgive us our sins and to cleanse us from all unrighteousness)1 John 1:7–9).

Old Testament View of Death

Genesis 4:8–10	Cain Kills Abel.
Genesis 4:16–24	Cain's genealogy and 2nd murder (4:23).
Genesis 4:26–5:1–32	The righteous line for the Redeemer through, literally, an obituary.
Genesis 5:24	Enoch did not join this obituary for God took him.
II Kings 2:1–11	Elijah taken to heaven in whirlwind.
Genesis 25:8	Abraham gathered unto his people.
Genesis 25.17	Ishmael gathered unto his people.
Genesis 35:29	Isaac gathered unto his people.
Genesis 49:33	Jacob (Israel) gathered unto his people.
Numbers 20:24	Aaron, Moses' brother, gathered unto his people.
Deuteronomy 32:48–52	Moses to die on Mount Nebo and be gathered to his people.
Judges 2:10	Generation of the nation of Israel.
II Kings 22:10	Josiah, righteous king, gathered to his fathers.

THE REVELATION OF LIFE AFTER DEATH BEFORE THE CROSS, AND AFTER THE CROSS

I Chronicles 17:11	David to go be with his fathers.
II Samuel 12:23	David to go to his dead son by Bathsbeba, But the son could not return to him.
Psalm 90:1	We fly away at death.
Psalm 89:48	Who shall not see death?
Ecclesiastes 3:19–21	Body of man and beast to turn to dust again.
Ecclesiastes 12:7	Spirit returns to God who gave it.
Ecclesiastes 8:8	Man has no power to retain the spirit at death.
Job 7:1	Is there not an appointed time to man on Earth?
Job 14:1–5	Days determined on the Earth?
Job 18:18	Wicked chased out the world from light into darkness.
Job 27:19	The rich man shall lie down (die), but he shall not be gathered: he openeth his eyes and he is not, (he is dead).
Proverbs 10:27	The fear of the Lord prolongeth days: but the years of the wicked shall be shortened.
Proverbs 14:27	The fear of the Lord is a fountain of life, to depart from the snares of death.
Proverbs 15:24	The way of life is above to the wise, that he may depart from hell beneath.

Scripture References for Drawings

1st Drawing	Luke 16:19–21W
2nd Drawing	Luke 16:22
3rd Drawing	Luke 16:22
4th Drawing	16:23–26
5th Drawing	16:27–28
6th Drawing	Luke 16:29–31
7th Drawing	Luke 23:39–41
8th Drawing	Matthew 12:40; Matthew 27:50–52; 1 Peter 3:18–1.9; 1 Peter 4:6
9th Drawing	Ephesians 4:8–12; Matthew 12:40; Acts 1:9–11
10th Drawing	Revelation 19:7–9; Revelation 6:11; Revelation 7:9; Revelation 7:13–17; 2 Corinthians 5:10
11th Drawing	Ephesians 2:8–10

THE REVELATION OF LIFE AFTER DEATH
BEFORE THE CROSS, AND AFTER THE CROSS

<u>Luke 16: 19–20</u> ¹⁹ There was a certain rich man, which was clothed in purple and fine linen, and fared sumptuously every day. ²⁰ And there was a certain beggar named Lazarus, which was laid at his gate, full of sores, ²¹ And desiring to be fed with the crumbs which fell from the rich man's table: moreover, the dogs came and licked his sores.

Notice that the dogs had more compassion for the beggar than the rich man. He evidently was very wealthy, dressed in fine clothes, and eating the best of food, but cared not for the poor or had any desire of helping someone in need. He probably had servants waiting on him. He could probably see the beggar from the window of his house. The dogs probably belonged to the rich man, but notice they did not bite the beggar, only licked his sores.

THE REVELATION OF LIFE AFTER DEATH BEFORE THE CROSS, AND AFTER THE CROSS

Luke 16:22

²² *And it came to pass, that the beggar died,* and was carried by the angels into Abraham's bosom: (Notice that at death Lazarus, a type of believer, had angelic escorts—more than one—who carried him into Abraham's bosom, the holding place for the righteous before Jesus died on the cross).

2 Corinthians 5:8	James 2:23
This side of the cross we are absent from the body and present with the Lord. Angels also escort us into the 3rd heaven, not to the heart of the Earth (Matthew 12:40)	Says this is Abraham, "He Was called the friend of God." Pretty awesome for God to say this of Abraham. Maybe this is why it is called Abraham's bosom?

Romans 4:3 *Abraham believed God,* and it was credited to him as righteousness. I believe this holding place was named after him because of his faith in God.

Hebrews 11:8 & 10 [8] *By faith Abraham, when he was called to go out into a place which he should after receive for an inheritance, obeyed; and he went out, not knowing whither he went.*
[10] *For he looked for a city which hath foundations, whose builder and maker is God.*

Luke 16:22(b)
[22(b)] *the rich man also died, and was buried.* Death is always the equalizer. In Hebrews 9:27, it is written, "And as it is appointed unto men once to die, but after this the judgement," Notice he did not have an angelic escort, but according to Job *18:18, the wicked are chased out of the world from light into darkness. Job 27:19–21,* [19] *The rich man shall lie down, but he shall not be gathered: he openeth his eyes, and he is not (he is dead).* [20] *Terrors take hold on him as waters, a tempest stealeth him away in the night.* [21] *The east wind carrieth him away, and he departeth: and as a storm hurleth him out of his place.* Can you imagine the horror and terror this rich man encountered at death? He probably believed that death ended it all or never even thought about death because riches were his god.

THE REVELATION OF LIFE AFTER DEATH BEFORE THE CROSS, AND AFTER THE CROSS

Luke 16:23–26 *²³ And in hell he lifts up his eyes, being in torments, and seeth Abraham afar off and Lazarus in his bosom. ²⁴ And he cried and said, Father Abraham, have mercy on me, and send Lazarus, that he may dip the tip of his finger in water, and cool my tongue; for I am tormented in this flame. ²⁵ But Abraham said, Son, remember that thou in thy lifetime receivedst thy good things, and likewise Lazarus evil things; but now he Is comforted, and thou art tormented. ²⁶ And beside all this, between us and you there is a great gulf fixed: so that they which would pass from hence to you cannot; neither can they pass to us, that would come from thence.*

Notice that after death, the <u>rich man</u> had his five senses still working (sight, mind, thirst, feeling, memory, etc.)

Definition: Abraham's Bosom is the holding place for the righteous from Adam to the death of Jesus on the cross. This holding place was changed from the heart of the earth to the third heaven after Jesus' payment for sin and set these souls free from this prison.

Both Lazarus and the rich man were prisoners except Lazarus was in comfort, and the rich man in torment. Jesus' death on the cross set Lazarus (a type of believer) free; whereas, the rich man (a type of unbeliever awaits the Great White Throne Judgement (Revelation 20: 11–15).

THE REVELATION OF LIFE AFTER DEATH
BEFORE THE CROSS, AND AFTER THE CROSS

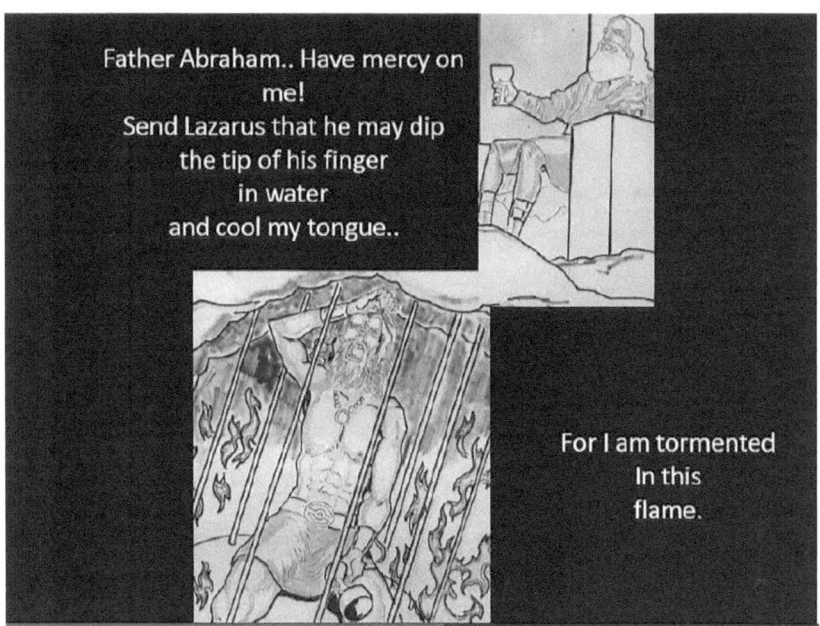

Luke 16:27–18 [27] *Then he said, I pray thee therefore, father, that thou wouldest send him to my father's house:* [28] *For I have five brethren; that he may testify unto them, lest they also come into this place of torment (hell).* This rich man now wants to be an evangelist from hell, because he knows his brothers have the same character as he had when he was alive on earth. No concern for the poor or their fellowman. Their riches have become their god. What about? Will you have someone in hell praying that you do not go there? Or do you trust that you are a good person, trust in your good works, the family you were born into, or your church attendance, and NOT Jesus and Him alone for your righteousness?

Luke 16:29–31 [29] *Abraham saith unto him, They have Moses' and the prophets; let them hear them.* [30] *And he said, Nay father Abraham: but if one went unto them from the dead, they will repent.* [31] *And he said unto him, If they hear not Moses and the prophets, neither will they be persuaded, though one rose from the dead.* Jesus did rise from the dead, and there are millions who will not repent and receive Jesus as Lord and Savior and will end up at death in the place of torment (hell).

THE REVELATION OF LIFE AFTER DEATH BEFORE THE CROSS, AND AFTER THE CROSS

Note: For believers today...*to be absent from the holy body is to be present with the Lord. (2 Corinthians 5:8)*

Luke 23:32 [32] *And there were also two other, malefactors, led with him to be put to death.*

Luke 23:39–49 [39] *And one of the malefactors which were hanged railed on him, saying, If thou be Christ, save thyself and us.* [40] *But the other answering rebuked him, saying, Dost not thou fear God, seeing thou art in the same condemnation?* [41] *And we indeed justly; for we receive the due reward of our deeds: but this man hath done nothing amiss.* [42] *And he said unto Jesus, Lord, remember me when thou comest into thy kingdom.* [43] *And Jesus said unto him, Verily I say unto thee, to day shalt thou be with me in paradise.*

The Crucifixion: The Payment for Sins

At death, the repentant thief was ushered into paradise (in the Old Testament—a holding place for believers) that was located (Matthew 12:40—For as Jonas was three days and three nights in the whale's belly; so shall the Son of man be three days and three nights in the heart of the earth.

This thief cried out to Jesus on the cross and was saved. What about you?

Matthew 12:40 ⁴⁰ For as Jonas was three days and three nights in the whale's belly; so shall the Son of man be three days and three nights in the heart of the earth.

Matthew 27:50–52 ⁵⁰ Jesus, when he had cried again with a loud voice, yielded up the ghost.

⁵¹And, behold, the veil of the temple was rent in twain from the top to the bottom; and the earth did quake, and the rocks rents;⁵²And the graves were opened; ⁵³ And came out of the graves after his resurrection, and went into the holy city, and appeared unto many.

1 Peter 3:18–19 ¹⁸ For Christ also hath once suffered for sins, the just for the unjust, that he might bring us to God, being put to death in the flesh, but quickened by the Spirit; ¹⁹ *By which also he went and preached unto the spirits in prison;*

1 Peter 4:6 ⁶ *For this cause was the gospel preached also to them that are dead, that they might be judged according to men in the flesh, but live according to God in the spirit.*

"The Descension"—Set the Captives Free

The Thief from the Cross   Believers Only Set Free From Prison

Ephesians 4:8 [8] *Wherefore he saith, When he ascended up on high, he led captivity (He set free the prisoners that were in Abraham's bosom—the Old Testament believers before the cross), and gave gifts unto men (for the church).*

Ephesians 4:11–12 [11]*And he gave some, apostles; and some, prophets; and some, evangelists; and some, pastors and teachers;* [12] *For the perfecting of the saints, for the work of the ministry, for the edifying of the body of Christ (the church—body of believers.)*

"The Ascension"—Led Captivity Captive

Ephesians 4:9
Now that he ascended what is it but that he also descended first into the lower parts of the earth?

Matthew 12:40
For as Jonas was three days and three nights in the whale's belly; so shall the Son of man be three days and three nights in the heart of the earth.

Ephesians 4:10
He that descended is the same also that ascended up far above all heavens, that he might fill all things.)

Acts 1:9–11
⁹ And when he had spoken these things, while they beheld, he was taken up; and a cloud received him out of their sight. ¹⁰ And while they looked steadfastly toward heaven as he went up, behold, two me stood by them in white apparel; ¹¹ Which also said, Ye men of Galilee, why stand ye gazing up into heaven? This same Jesus, which is taken up from you into heaven, shall so come in like manner as ye have seen him go into heaven.

The Rapture

The English word *"rapture"* comes from the Latin word *"rapere"* which means *to snatch away; to be caught up;* or since I know who is doing the catching or snatching away, I call it a "blissful seizure." The Old Testament records two people that were snatched, blissfully seized, or caught up. The first was a righteous man named Enoch who never died for God took him (Genesis 5:24.) Later the Bible tells us that the prophet Elijah also escaped death when he was taken up by a whirlwind into heaven (2 Kings 2:11), who I believe will be the two witnesses of Revelation 11:3–12. Notice in Verse 11–12 they are caught up into heaven also. [11] *And after three days and a half the spirit of life from God entered into them, and they stood upon their feet, and great fear fell upon them which saw them. These two men's bodies had lain in the street for three and one-half days after the beast that had ascended out of the Bottomless Pit had killed them. And they see them raised to their feet.* [12] *And they heard a great voice from heaven saying unto them* (the two witnesses), *Come up hither. And they ascended up to heaven in a cloud, and their enemies beheld them.* They were raptured off the earth to heaven as their enemies were affrighted because of all the things that took place, Revelation 11:13. The apostle Paul sheds additional light on the rapture in this first letter to the Thessalonians 4:13–18 [13] *But I would not have you to be ignorant, brethren concerning them which are asleep (dead), that ye sorrow not, even as others which have no hope.* [14] *For if we believe that Jesus died and rose again, even so them also which sleep (dead) in Jesus will God bring with him.* [15] *For this we say unto you by the word of the Lord, that we which are alive and remain unto the coming of the Lord shall not prevent (go before) them which are asleep (dead).* [16] *For the Lord himself shall descend from heaven with a shout, with the voice of the archangel, and with the trump of God: and the dead in Christ shall rise first:* ¹⁷ *Then we which are alive and remain shall be caught up together with them in the clouds, to meet the Lord in the air: and so shall we ever be with the Lord.* ¹⁸ *Wherefore comfort one another these words.*

This represents a generation that will be alive at Christ's return for His church (believers—not a denomination or building) that will pass from this earthly life to life eternal without passing through the portals of death, 1 Corinthians 15:51–56 ⁵¹ *Behold, I shew you a mystery; We shall not all sleep (be dead), but we shall all be changed,* ⁵² *In a moment, in the twinkling of an eye (as fast as you can blink), at the last trump: for the trumpet shall sound, and the dead shall be raised incorruptible (fit for heaven), and we shall be changed.* ⁵³ *For this corruptible (believers dead in the grave) must put on incorruption, and this mortal (living believers) must put on immortality (eternal body).* ⁵⁴ *So when this corruptible (dead in Christ) shall have put on incorporation, and this mortal (living believers) shall have put on immortality, then shall be brought to pass the saying that is written, Death is swallowed up in victory.* ⁵⁵ *O death, where is thy sitting? O grave, where is thy victory?* ⁵⁶ *The sting of death is sin (cause); and the strength of sin is the law (because the law reveals sin).* This transformation allows us to enter into heaven. 1 Corinthians 15:50 *Now this I say, brethren, that flesh and blood cannot inherit (enter) the kingdom of God; neither doth corruption (death) inherit (obtain) incorruption.*

The Rapture

We have to go through a transformation to enter into the heavenly kingdom of God (1 Corinthians 15:44) it is sown (at death) a natural body; it is raised a spiritual body, (eternal body). If believers are not raptured and transformed, they would have to spend eternity in heaven without a body. We all (believers) must receive a new spiritual body to enjoy all that Christ has prepared for us in Heaven. Therefore, the promise to the church (believer), is that we will all be changed, transformed the dead in Christ and living (believers), at the moment of His coming, both groups simultaneously as they are raptured from the earth. Those who take part in the rapture will then appear before Christ's judgement seat to receive the things done in his body (natural, earthly), according to that he had done whether it be good or bad, but not for salvation, but for rewards or crowns (1 Corinthians 5:10). There is a difference of opinions between theologians as the timing of the rapture, whether Pre-tribulation, Mid-tribulation, or Post-tribulation. However, the Bible urges believers to place their primary focus on Christ's return not on their martyrdom or suffering, but to wait for His Son from heaven, whom He raised from the dead, even Jesus, (notice this) who delivered us from the wrath to come in 1 Peter 3:20 God saved Noah, his wife, his three sons, and their wives, eight souls by water (above the flood). And spared not the old worlds, but saved Noah the eighth person, a preacher of righteousness, bringing in the flood upon the world of the ungodly (2 Peter 2:5). *By faith Noah, being warned of God of things not seen as yet, moved with fear, prepared an ark to the saving of his house; by the which he condemned the world* (Noah's faith was vindicated, and the world's unbelief was judged, bringing the flood on the whole earth) Hebrews 11:4. God also delivered the children of Israel thought the Red Sea, but drowned Pharaoh and his army in the Red Sea and not on Israelite perished. In Psalm 106:7–11 The children of Israel[7]...provoked him at the sea, even at the Red Sea. [8]Nevertheless he saved them for his name's sake, that he might make His mighty power to be known. [9]He rebuked the Red Sea also, and it was dried up: so he led them through the depths (of the Red Sea), as though the wilderness. [10] And he saved them from the hand of him that hated them, and redeemed them from the hand of the enemy (pharaoh and his army). [11]And the waters covered their enemies (only after the children of Israel made it to the other side of the Red Sea): there was not one of them left. God delivered Noah above the flood waters, the children of Israel through the waters of the Red Sea, and then there is Lot whom God delivered out of Sodom, Gomorrah, Admah, and Zeboim, the cities of the plain whom the Lord rained fire and brimstone from heaven, in his anger and wrath (Genesis 19:24–25, and Deuteronomy 29:23. Notice that he, his two daughters, and his wife were delivered out of Sodom and Gomorrah before the towns were destroyed, safely removing them from the wrath to come. 1 Thessalonians 1:10 describes how the Thessalonians turned from idols to living God. ¹⁰ And to wait for his Son from heaven, whom he raised from the dead, even Jesus, which delivered us from the wrath to come. Lot's wife looked back and turned to a pillar of salt.

In all of the examples that are listed in the Holy Bible, God always removed the righteous before he poured out His wrath and punishment. That is the reason I hold to a Pre-tribulation rapture that if you are a believer redeemed by the blood of Christ, you are a purchased possession, and you can go with us, too.

The picture shown on the next page is an artist's drawing of the "rapture."

Revelation 19:17–9 ⁷ *Let us be glad and rejoice, and give honour to him: for the marriage of the Lamb has come, and his wife bath made herself ready.* ⁸*And to her was granted that she should be arrayed in fine linen, clean and white: for the fine linen is the righteousness of saints. And he saith unto me, Write, Blessed are they which are called unto the marriage supper of the Lamb.*

And he saith unto me, These are the true sayings of God.

(This picture is from an unknown source)

THE REVELATION OF LIFE AFTER DEATH BEFORE THE CROSS, AND AFTER THE CROSS

The "Arrival"—Led the Believers from the Heart of the Earth to the 3rd Heaven

White robes given to them (Revelation 6:11, Revelation 7:9, Revelation 19:8).

2 Corinthians 5:10—for believers only: *For we must all appear before the judgment seat of Christ; that everyone may receive the things done in his body, according to that he hath done, whether it be good or bad.*

Ephesians 2:8–9 [8] *For by grace are ye saved through faith; and that not of yourselves: it is the gift of God:* [9] *Not of works, lest any man should boast.* John 19:30, *When Jesus therefore had received the vinegar, he said, It is finished: and he bowed his head, and gave up the ghost* (He died). Jesus had paid the price for salvation, for all those who would by faith put their trust in the finished work on the cross for sin and receive

His free gift of eternal life, found only in Jesus and Him alone, for the redemption of those who accept His payment. Please don't be deceived into thinking your good works, character, and deeds will be enough to earn your entrance into heaven. God requires absolute holiness that only Jesus had. *The blood of Christ cleanses us from all sin (1 John 1:7).*

"The Victory"—It is Finished

If you don't know or have not accepted Jesus as your Lord and Savior, I would have you to pray this prayer to God

"Heavenly Father, I'm a sinner in need of a Savior. I believe that Jesus died on the cross for my sin and on the third day He arose from the dead with all power in His hands. I, now repent of my sins, and ask you, Jesus, to come into my heart in the person of the Holy Spirit and be my Lord and Savior. In Jesus' name. Amen."

THE REVELATION OF LIFE AFTER DEATH BEFORE THE CROSS, AND AFTER THE CROSS

If you prayed this prayer from your heart, and meant it, welcome to the family of God. It is written in 2 Corinthians 5:21 that, *For he hath made him to be sin for us, who knew no sin; that we might be made the righteousness of God in him.* (Jesus). Are you in Jesus and Jesus in you? The next pages of this book describe all those who depend on their works for salvation, and not Jesus and the judgment that follows. If they depend on their works, they are not listed in the Lamb's book of life. The next page shows the works of the believer and the judgment for rewards and crowns at the judgment seat of Christ, believers only. The book of life and Lamb's book of life are given as a possible example of the book of life. Only God knows the exact replica.

Please respond to the most important page of the whole book. Then I say please respond to the prayer of this whole page and have your name written in the lamb's Book of Life example on page 43.

Book of Works
"Apart from Christ"

Isaiah 64:6 ⁶ But we are all as an unclean thing, and all our righteousnesses are as filthy rags…

"The Great White Throne Judgment" (For Unbelievers Only)

Revelation 20:11–15 *¹¹ And I saw a great white throne, and him that sat on it, from whose face the earth and the heaven fled away; and there was found no place for them. ¹² And I saw the dead, small and great, stand before God; and the books were opened: and another book was opened, which is the book of life: and the dead were judged out of those things which were written in the books, according to their "works." ¹³ And the sea gave up the dead which were in it; and death and hell delivered up the dead which were in them: and they were judged every man according to their "works."* They were standing on their own "works" and merits instead of Christ's imputed righteousness given to all who put their trust in His works. *¹⁴ And death and hell were cast into the lake of fire. This is the second death. ¹⁵ And whosoever was not found written in the book of life was cast into the lake of fire.* Please, before it is too late eternally, repent of your sins and turn to Jesus for salvation and your eternal home.

Not for Salvation
Works for the Believer and Reward

1 Corinthians 3:11–15 *[11] For other foundation can no man lay than that is laid, which is Jesus Christ.* [12] *Now if any man build upon this foundation* (for Christ) *gold, silver, precious stones, wood, hay, stubble* (things done for your own glory); [13] *Every man's work shall be made manifest: for the day shall declare it, because it shall be revealed by fire; and the fire shall try every man's work of what sort it is.* Fire will purify gold, silver, or precious stones, but wood, hay, and stubble will burn up after being put in the fire. [14] *If any man's work abide which he hath built thereupon, he shall receive a reward.* [15] *If any man's work shall be burned, he shall suffer loss: but he himself shall be saved; yet so as by fire.* This is only for those who put their trust and faith in Jesus alone. Thank you, Lord Jesus.

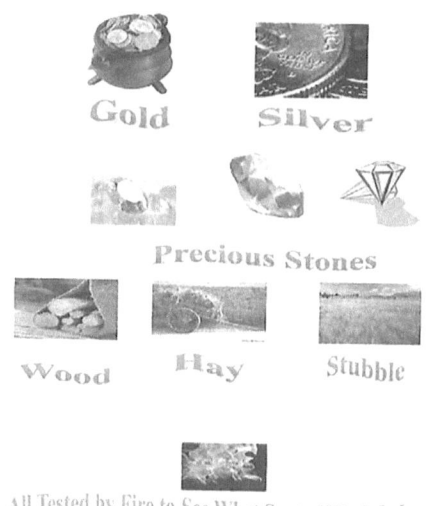

All Tested by Fire to See What Sort of Work It Is.

Crowns and Rewards for Believers

[For Believers Only] Rewards and Crowns are Awaiting You and Me

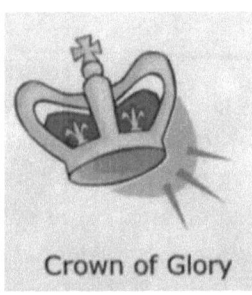
Crown of Glory

1. **<u>Crown of Glory</u>**: For Faithful Servants, *we shall receive a crown of glory that fadeth not away*. (1 Peter 5:4) Those who have served Jesus Christ as elders and pastors in the church will receive their reward from God. Though they have often not received any thanks for their time and resources here on earth, they shall receive a crown of glory.

Crown of Rejoicing

2. **<u>Crown of Rejoicing for Soul Winners</u>**: For what is our hope or crown of rejoicing? (1 Thessalonians 2:19). Those who have won others to faith in Jesus Christ as their Savior will experience joy because these new believers are their spiritual children, and they receive this reward in heaven.

Crown of Righteousness

3. **<u>Crown of Righteousness</u>**: For those who love His return, 2 Timothy 4:8 tells us, *Henceforth there is laid up for me a crown of righteousness, which the Lord, the righteous judge, shall give me at that day: and not to me only, but unto all them also that love his appearing.* This crown will be given to those who long for the return of Christ, being watchful for the imminent return of Jesus Christ.

Incorruptible Crown

4. **Incorruptible Crown**: For victorious lives of purity, *And every man that striveth for the mastery is temperate in all things. Now they do it to obtain a corruptible crown; but we an incorruptible (1 Corinthians 9:25).* Paul encourages us to put on the whole armour of God (Ephesians 6:11). Those who do put on the whole armor of God, will receive an incorruptible crown.

Crown of Life

5. **Crown of Life**: For Christian martyrs, Christ promises a crown of life for all saints through the ages who have suffered martyrdom for their faith in Him (Revelation 2:10).

Book of Remembrance **Malachi 3:16**	**Lambs Book of Life** **Revelation 13:8; 21:27**
Abel Righteous	Abel
Cain	**Blotted Out**
Righteous Wicked	Adam
Adam	Eve
Eve	Seth
Seth	**Blotted Out**
Jezebel Wicked	**Blotted Out**
Ahab Wicked	Noah
Noah	Baby John
Baby John (Miscarriage)	Baby Jessica
Baby Jessica (Aborted)	Infant Michael
Infant Michael (Murdered,	Abraham
Abraham	Isaac
Isaac	Jacob
Jacob	Zacchaeus
Zacchaeus (Tax Collector)	**Blotted Out**
Hitler	**Blotted Out**
M. O'Hara (Atheist)	**Blotted Out**
Saddam Hussein	Billy Graham
Billy Graham	Mother Teresa
Mother Teresa	**Blotted Out**
You (Is this You?)	You
You (Or is This You?)	

The Heavenly City
New Jerusalem

In John 14:1–6 Jesus, describes a place with many mansions that are being prepared for people who believe in God and believe also in Him. And that He would return again and receive you unto himself that where He is you may be also. And we do not have to worry about how do I get there? Jesus says, *"I am the way, the truth, and the life: no man cometh unto the Father, but by me."* The world of unbelievers would say that there are many ways to God and heaven, but Jesus states in John 14:6 that He is the only way to this heavenly city. The largest percentage of teaching about heaven in the New Testament consists of information about the heavenly city, the New Jerusalem. The capital city of heaven is filled with God's glory and glows with an eternal light, *even like jasper stone, clear as crystal* (Revelation 21:11). New Jerusalem is an enormous city, 1,500 miles long on each side. Its foundation wall is over 216 feet high, and it has twelve gates with twelve layers of stone supporting the foundation that is made of precious stones like jasper, sapphire, emerald, topaz, amethyst, and others as described in Revelation 21:19–20. Also, before I forget, the gates were made of twelve pearls. The streets in the New Jerusalem are made of pure gold, transparent like glass (Revelation 21:21).
There will be no need of the sun or moon to provide light in the New Jerusalem because the *glory of God did lighten it, and the Lamb* (Jesus) is the light thereof Revelation 21:23. *And the nations of them which are saved shall walk in the light of it; and the gates of it shall not be shut at all by day: for there shall be no night there.* Do you want to know why the gates will never be closed or locked? *And there shall in no wise enter into it anything that defileth, neither whatsoever worketh*

abomination, or maketh a lie: but they which are written in the Lamb's book of life (Revelation 21:27). The only way into this Holy City is JESUS, JESUS, JESUS.

These twelve gates, with twelve angels have the names of the twelve tribes of the children of Israel written thereon (Revelation 21:12). Also the foundations have in them the names of the twelve apostles of the Lamb (Revelation 21:14). Only God knows the true heart of any person. Unless we truly repent, turn from our sinful rebellion and accept Christ as our Lord and Savior, we shall never experience the salvation of Christ and have our names recorded in the Lamb's Book of life. No amount of good works or theological knowledge will qualify us to enter through these gates. The only acceptable price of salvation and pardon from the Lake of Fire, (Revelation 20:15), is the blood Christ shed on the Cross for each one of us who receives this free gift of eternal life.

In my Father's house are many mansions…(John 14:1) These mansions will pale in comparison to the mansion you will have in New Jerusalem.

THE REVELATION OF LIFE AFTER DEATH, BEFORE THE CROSS + AND AFTER THE CROSS † AS REVEALED BY JESUS IN LUKE 16:19–31.

It is my desire to relate what the Old Testament revealed about death before the cross from Genesis to Ecclesiastes and what happens to a believer and unbeliever after the cross, as well as the different judgments, destinations, and rewards in heaven for believers. As believers, we look for a new heaven, a new earth, and a new Jerusalem with God Himself being with us as believers. (Revelation 21:1–3)

Summary

So, before we close out this last chapter, let's see where we are on God's prophetic timetable. I believe and not only me, there are many Biblical scholars that would come to this same conclusion, that we are in the last days of the time of the Gentiles and the church age. We are living in a period just prior to the Rapture which has been previously described. Nothing else prophetically speaking has to occur before the Rapture occurs; as it can happen at any time, but in God's timing. Since flesh and blood cannot inherit the Kingdom of God, 1 Corinthians 15:50. We have to get a glorified body made of flesh and bone, Luke 24:39, where Jesus says, "behold my hand and my feet, that it is I myself, handle me and see for a spirit hath not flesh and bone as you see me have." Notice, He did not say flesh and blood, but flesh and bones. 1 John 3:2 says, "beloved now are we the sons of God and it doth not yet appear what we shall be, be we know that, when he shall appear, we shall be like him; for we shall see Him as He is." At this resurrection, Jesus' physical body went through a transformation, where his body was and made of flesh and bone. For those that believe that our present bodies will have no relationship to our resurrection bodies, we have only to look at Jesus' resurrection. The body He had was the same body He was crucified in, only glorified. Besides all this, the Bible talks about a bodily resurrection. 1 Corinthians 15:35–38 says, [35] But some man will say how are the dead raised up? [36] Thou fool, that which you sowest (your dead body) is not quickened (made alive) except it die; [37] and that which thou sowest (your dead body to the grave) not that body that shall be, but bare grain, it may chance of wheat, or some other grain. [38] But God giveth it a body (resurrection) as it hath please Him, and to every seed his own body. Don't be afraid that our bodies will still be old and worn out because Philippians 3:20–21 says, "[20] For our conversation is in heaven; from whence also we look for the Saviour, the Lord Jesus Christ:

[21] Who shall change our vile body, that it may be fashioned like unto his glorious body, according to the working whereby he is able even to subdue all things unto himself." Jesus was thirty–three years old when he died. I John 3:2 says," we shall be like Him." It is very likely that we will have young resurrection glorified bodies. We will be in heaven in glorified resurrection bodies and stand before the Judgment Seat of Christ. 2 Corinthians 5:10 says, "[10] For we must all (believers only) appear before the judgment seat of Christ; that everyone may receive the things done in his body, according to that he hath done, whether it be good or bad." This judgment is for rewards and privileges because our sins were taken away at the cross. The next event is the tribulation period of seven years, the last three and one–half years are considered to be the Great Tribulation because of the intensity and severity of the judgments. Brothers and sisters, it will be evil at its zenith. During this period, God is mainly dealing with the nation of Israel and their heart, although Gentiles that did not trust in Jesus will go through this terrible time of human history. All nations come to destroy Israel off the face of the earth. Just before they are able to do this to the nation of Israel, the Lord Jesus rescues them from destruction. In Revelation 19:15, the Bible says of Jesus against these nations coming against Israel–[15] And out of his mouth goeth a sharp sword, that with it he should smite the nations: and he shall rule them with a rod of iron: and he treadeth the winepress of the fierceness and wrath of Almighty God. Revelation 14:20 says, 20 And the winepress was trodden without the city, and blood came out of the winepress, even unto the horse bridles, by the space of a thousand and six hundred furlongs. (The approximate length of the Holy Land from north to south).

In Matthew 25:31–34, Jesus after the tribulation has been completed, separates the sheep from the goats (those who will enter the millennial kingdom on earth in natural bodies. The sheep (believers) go into the kingdom, and the goats (unbelievers) go to everlasting punishment. (Matthew 25:46). Satan and his cohorts are bound in the bottomless pit for the thousand-year reign of Christ on the earth (Revelation 20:1–3) that he should not deceive the nations no more, till the thousand years should be fulfilled and after this he must be loosed a little season, and shall go out to deceive the nations which are in the four quarters of the earth (north, south, east and west) to gather them together to battle. Satan deceives the nations to rise to fight against the Christ and the Saints in the beloved city. These people will be off-spring of the believers at the start of the millennial reign of Christ that had natural bodies. Believers in glorified bodies—Hey, that's us!—are also in this beloved city. This is Satan's last attempt to thwart God's plans and is cast into the lake of Fire where the beast, (antichrist), and the false prophet were cast a thousand years earlier (Revelation 19:20 and Revelation 20:10). Search out these scriptures given. The beast (the antichrist) and the false prophet are and shall be tormented day and night forever and ever. The beast and false prophet were cast in the Lake of Fire one thousand years— earlier at the end of the Tribulation Period (Revelation 19:20). Can you imagine living under the perfect rule of Jesus Christ for one thousand years and choose to side with the devil. I guess Genesis 8:21 is indeed right, for the imagination of man's heart is evil from his youth. Jeremiah 17:9 tells us that, The heart is deceitful above all things, and desperately wicked: who can know it? So, is the heart of man that has not been born again from above and led by the spirit of the living God. So, don't look too harshly at Adam and Eve. What would we have done? The next prophetic event is the Great White Throne Judgment which is for all those who have not been cleansed from their sins by the shed blood of Christ on the cross and did not get recorded in the Lambs Book of Life. They stand before God on the merits of their own works. Boy, are they in for a rude awakening. Everyone at this judgment is cast into the Lake of Fire. This is the second death, Revelation 20:14. The next event on the prophetic calendar is a new heaven and a new earth; then the eternal state, where we're with Jesus forever and ever and ever because the first heaven and earth were passed away and there was no more sea. Revelation

THE REVELATION OF LIFE AFTER DEATH
BEFORE THE CROSS, AND AFTER THE CROSS

21:2 says, And I, John saw that the Holy City, New Jerusalem coming down from God out of heaven, prepared as a bride adorned for her husband.

Literally, heaven and earth becomes one. Like a husband and bride become one. Heaven moves from the third heaven to earth. This is awesome in itself. God will tabernacle with men and will dwell with them and God himself will be their God.

God promises to wipe away all tears from their eyes, no more death, neither sorrow, nor crying, neither shall there be any more pain: for the former things are passed away. Hallelujah!

Then we enter into eternity with our God forever and ever and ever. Bless His name. Hallelujah, thank you Lord Jesus.

www.ingramcontent.com/pod-product-compliance
Lightning Source LLC
LaVergne TN
LVHW041716060526
838201LV00043B/769